ALMOST FILIPINO

FILIPINO RECIPES STYLED BY A
STATESIDE CHILDHOOD

By Liezel de La Isla

Published by LZL BOOKS

Almost Filipino

Copyright © 2021 by Liezel de La Isla.

Photographs © Liezel de La Isla

Front and Back Cover design © Liezel de La Isla

All rights reserved. No part of this publication may be reproduced, distributed or transmitted in any form or by any means, including photocopying, recording, or other electronic or mechanical methods, without the prior written permission of the publisher, except in the case of brief quotations embodied in critical reviews and certain other noncommercial uses permitted by copyright law. For permission requests, write to the publisher, addressed "Attention: Permissions Coordinator," at the email address below.

de La Isla, Liezel / LZL Books
JLDIBOOKS@gmail.com

Ordering Information:

Quantity sales. Special discounts are available on quantity purchases by corporations, associations, and others. For details, contact the "Special Sales Department" at the email address above.

Almost Filipino/ Liezel de La Isla. —1st ed.
ISBN 978-0-578-32783-9

CONTENTS

INTRODUCTION 5
HEAVY ON ROTATION 7
DID SOMEONE SAY PARTY? 27
SWEET CRAVINGS 39

Almost Filipino

For my parents, Oca and Precy-*Maraming salamat po!* And to my daughters, Tala and Pau, for the day that you will want to take these flavors and memories into your own kitchens.

Introduction

"Kumain ka na ba?"

Did you eat yet? In my family, these exact words would embrace my brothers and I as soon as we walked through the door. Inside the kitchen, our mother would be hovering over the stove with a metal spoon, stirring up our *ulam*. The aroma drifting from the kitchen would give us hints about tangy *adobo*, citrusy *sinigang*, or pungent *sinangag* for dinner. She would look up from her cooking, turn to us and ask *"Kumain ka na ba?"* On the frequent visits to the home of our grandmother and aunts, the words *"Kumain ka na ba?"* would ring through the air, as soon as we passed through the door. Lingering behind that greeting would be a pot of jasmine rice, warm in the rice cooker, and some *sinigang* with shrimp or gingery *arroz caldo* simmering on the stovetop. This is just one of the ways my family shows love.

My parents moved from the Philippines to the US in the 1970s and ended up settling in Queens, New York. This diverse city became the place of my birth, as well as the playground of my youth and young adult years. Within the walls of my family's home, we were sprinkled with a mix of Filipino and American cultures, but growing up I never quite felt American or Filipino enough. Interestingly, I experienced this same feeling when I would visit the Philippines. Despite this sometimes uncomfortable tension, the one thing that definitely tied me to my Filipino roots were the dishes made by my family-from my *Lola* (Grandmother) to my *'Nay* (mom) to my *Titas* (aunts) and, at times, even my dad.

Looking back, I can clearly remember being surrounded by so much vibrant cooking. Our kitchen tables were always bustling with activity, whether it was preparing a meal or eating one, the kitchen was an area of the house that was rarely vacant. My aunt chopping garlic and frying it in pans, the careful hands of my grandmother and mom working side by side while rolling *lumpia*, or my father grating coconut from its shell, are a few of the scenes that I fondly remember from our kitchen. However, what I can't recall ever witnessing is anyone in our family using a recipe or a measuring tool!

Almost Filipino

When I left home, the only cooking appliance that I packed in my shipment was a rice cooker. Yep, I was a good Filipino girl. I knew how to make rice and basically thought that I was ready for the world! But as the distance and time apart grew longer, homesickness crept in and the only way I could treat the malaise was to indulge in the flavors of my childhood. From my shared apartment in Milan, I remember making plenty of long distance phone calls to my family, asking how to replicate my favorite Filipino dishes. However, the directions dictated to me were often confusing and challenging to follow. I was in search of recipes and exact measurements, but instead I got "add a little bit of this," or "put it in and boil it all together," and heard plenty of "until it tastes right!" This led to a ton of cooking experiments gone wrong.

Living outside of the Philippines and NYC also made learning how to cook Filipino food problematic. Unlike Queens, which had an abundance of Asian grocery stores, I moved to places that lacked access to the products I needed. I learned to substitute tamarind for lemons, watercress for spinach or okra for green beans. With every new city or country, I immediately sought out the closest Asian market. Some of them required making a "field trip" where I hoped to find *lumpia* wrappers, *ube* or *patis*. Not every expedition turned out to be successful, so, after every trip back home, I made sure to return with a suitcase packed with these "exotic" ingredients.

Leaving the nest forced me to learn how to cook Filipino food, or what I like to call "Almost Filipino." Capturing the flavors and reliving the memories of my family's kitchens provides me with great comfort during times of separation. It also made me realize how much I enjoy the act of cooking and sharing food. Over the years, this has grown to become a healthy obsession of mine. Eventually with a lot of practice, I am now excitedly ready to present "a little bit of this" and "until it tastes just right," together in a way that comes close to my experiences with Filipino food.

This cookbook highlights some of the recipes that regularly appeared on the dining tables of my childhood, and are the dishes requested nowadays by my own children. Also included are some recipes that are often featured during Filipino celebrations, as well as a few treats to satisfy any sweet tooth! Hopefully, this little guide will support your interest in cooking Filipino food at home, especially if, like me, you've never lived in the Philippines. These recipes are based on my family's adaptations from when they moved from the Philippines to the US and on my own changes, after recreating them in Europe, where I continue to cook "Almost Filipino." Thank you for choosing this book and I hope you'll enjoy these household favorites! *Kain na tayo*! (Let's eat!)

HEAVY ON ROTATION

The following recipes are what I would call "everyday" dishes. They can be enjoyed anytime during the week or weekends -for lunch or dinner- and usually, with rice on the side.

Let's start with the almighty rice! This is my preferred way to make rice because it always comes out perfect and it's never a true Filipino meal without some rice on the side!

Rice
SERVES 4-5

Ingredients:

2 cups of jasmine rice

2 cups water

pinch of salt

drop of olive oil

Equipment:

1 rice cooker

measuring cup

Instructions:

1. Measure and pour the cups of rice into the rice cooker.

2. Then rinse the rice with water from the tap.

3. Strain it and return the rice to the pot.

4. Add 2 cups of water to the rice, as well as the salt and olive oil.

5. Then place the pot in the rice cooker and turn on the machine according to its instructions.

Got leftover rice? Make this....
Growing up, we often enjoyed this rice with fried eggs and some chopped tomatoes or ketchup for breakfast!

Sinangag (Garlic Fried Rice)
SERVES 4-6

Ingredients:

1-2 tablespoons of minced garlic

1 tablespoon of oil

2 cups of leftover rice

salt to taste

Optional: 1-2 scallions, chopped

Instructions:

1. Heat up a large frying pan or wok.

2. Add the oil.

3. When the oil is hot, add the garlic.

4. On low-medium heat, stir and cook until golden.

5. Then add the leftover rice. Using a wooden spoon, break down the rice and mix in the garlic. Stir for a couple of minutes and then serve immediately with or without chopped scallions.

The following are suggestions for different variations of sinangag:

Veggie Fried Rice: When adding the rice, add ¾ cup of frozen vegetables such as peas, carrots or corn.

Veggie Fried Rice with Eggs: After step 5, beat two eggs in a bowl, make a well in the center of the pan and then pour in the eggs. When the bottom looks firm, use a wooden spoon to break up the egg and mix it into the rice.

Fried rice with veggies and bacon or sausage: Before adding the garlic, heat the pan with a little bit of oil, then cook the diced bacon or chopped sausage. Then with a slotted spoon, remove it and then cook the rest of the ingredients in the leftover fat. After step 5, return the meat to the dish, cook until it is heated through and serve immediately.

A little twist on the Philippines "national" dish. My kids especially enjoy the bite size style of these chicken wings!

Chicken Adobo Wings
SERVES 6

Ingredients:

2 pounds chicken wings

1 garlic head, crushed

½ cup white vinegar

¼ cup soy sauce

½ tablespoon whole peppercorns

1-2 bay leaves

1 tablespoon coconut or brown sugar

Optional: ½ cup of coconut milk

Instructions:

1. Place all the ingredients, except for the sugar and coconut milk, into a large pot. Coat the chicken evenly with the sauce.

2. Heat up the mixture and let it come to a boil.

3. When it is boiling, turn down the heat and let it cook for 30 or more minutes.

4. When it is almost ready, heat the broiler with an oven rack about 6 inches away from the heat.

5. Line a baking sheet with foil. With a slotted spoon, remove the chicken from the pot and place them on the baking sheet, skin side up.

6. When the oven is ready, broil the chicken for 5-8 minutes or until the skin looks crisp.

7. Strain the sauce from the pot, discard the pepper and garlic. Return the liquid to the pot, add the sugar and allow it to reduce and thicken. If using coconut milk, you may also add it in now.

8. When the chicken is ready, move it to a serving platter and drizzle the sauce on top. Serve with rice and a salad of chopped tomatoes with thin slices of red onions. Drizzle salad with white vinegar and salt.

Torta in our family meant "cooked in an omelette form." There are so many different variations of *torta*. I've only included two in this book, but in reality the options are endless!

Torta (Tomato and Onion Omelette)
SERVES 4

Ingredients:

4 eggs

2 cloves garlic, chopped

1 onion, chopped

1 tomato, chopped

Instructions:

1. Heat 2 tablespoons of oil.

2. Fry the garlic until golden brown. Then add the onions and tomatoes. Let it cook for a few minutes under low-medium heat.

3. While the vegetables are cooking, crack the four eggs into a bowl and beat well.

4. When the vegetables are completely cooked through, use a slotted spoon to scoop out the mixture and add it to the eggs. Quickly incorporate the ingredients well.

5. Place a drop of oil in the pan and return the entire mixture to it and cook on low heat.

6. After a few minutes, the bottom of the omelette should be firm. With a plate larger than the pan, place it over the pan. Then holding the plate firmly with one hand, invert the pan. Then slide the omelette back on to the pan and cook until done.

Enjoy with some bread or with some garlic fried rice on the side.

Torta Special (Mix Veggie Omelette)
(MAKES ABOUT 24 SMALL-MEDIUM SIZED PATTIES OF *TORTA*)

Ingredients:

8 medium-sized potatoes, peeled and chopped into small pieces

8 cloves of garlic, minced

½ tomato, diced

1 large onion, diced

7 medium-sized eggs

½ red pepper, diced

½ green pepper, diced

2 to 3 tablespoons of olive oil

salt and pepper to taste

Instructions:

1. Heat oil in a large pan.

2. On low-medium heat, add garlic, onion, tomatoes and let it cook for about 5-7 minutes.

3. Then add the potatoes.

4. Stir well and cook until potatoes are tender, about 20 minutes.

5. Meanwhile, beat the eggs in a large bowl.

6. Add the chopped pepper to the bowl of eggs and mix.

7. When the vegetable mixture is ready, let it cool down for a few minutes. Taste and season to your liking with salt and black pepper. (Allowing the mixture to cool will prevent the eggs from curdling in the next step.)

8. When it has cooled, add it to the eggs and pepper.

9. Blend together thoroughly.

10. Heat a large non-stick frying pan.

11. On low-medium heat, add a few drops of oil and then add about ¼ cup of the mixture into the pan.

12. When the bottom firms up, use a spatula to carefully flip the *torta* over.

13. Repeat until all the batter is finished.

Enjoy with a plate of rice and chopped tomatoes with a sprinkle of salt or as the Filipina kid in me enjoys it, with a side of banana ketchup! If that is not available, regular tomato ketchup works too.

Almost Filipino

This is the ultimate bowl of comfort food! It got my brothers and I through cold season, and whenever we were feeling a bit under the weather, this dish helped us quickly bounce back.

Lola's Arroz Caldo
SERVES 6-8

Ingredients:

1 whole chicken, cut into pieces

1/4 cup of thinly sliced ginger

10 cloves garlic, minced

1 onion, chopped

3-4 tablespoons of vegetable oil

1-2 scallions, chopped

1-2 tablespoons of patis (fish sauce)

1 cup of sweet glutinous rice

1 cup of jasmine rice

10-12 cups of water

few strands of saffron

salt and pepper to taste

Instructions:

1. In a large pot, heat oil and add the minced garlic and ginger under low-medium heat.

2. Cook until slightly golden.

3. Add onion, cook until translucent.

4. When the onion is soft, add the chicken.

5. Turn heat down to low and continue to sauté for about 15 minutes. The chicken should "sweat" and will start to add some juices to the mixture.

6. Then add both types of rice and the *patis*.

7. Afterwards, add 10 cups of water for a thick porridge. For a thinner type of porridge, use 12 cups of water.

8. Add saffron.

9. Increase the heat and allow the water to come to a boil. When it does, bring the porridge down to a simmer.

10. Cook for about 30-40 minutes. Stir occasionally, to prevent the rice from sticking to the bottom of the pot.

11. Season to taste with salt, pepper or more *patis*. Garnish with crispy garlic bits (see below), chopped scallions, extra fish sauce, sliced lemons, soy sauce or a combination of any of these condiments.

Crispy Garlic Topping: Peel and mince a whole head of garlic. In a frying pan, heat up some oil and then add the minced garlic. On low heat, fry until golden brown. Then with a slotted spoon, remove and place in a strainer lined with a paper towel. Let cool. Serve in a small bowl and any leftover can be stored in an airtight container.

Almost Filipino

This is my go-to for when I'm craving something quick and easy! It's great with rice, chopped tomatoes and drizzled with some dipping sauce (below)!

Pan Fried Tofu
SERVES 4

Ingredients:

1 large block of tofu, cubed

4 tablespoons cornstarch or flour

1 sandwich bag

1 teaspoon salt

Instructions:

1. Place cornstarch, salt and tofu cubes in the bag.

2. Shake the bag and be sure to coat the tofu well with the cornstarch.

3. Heat up 1-2 tablespoons of oil.

4. On low-medium heat, add the coated pieces of tofu and fry until golden on all sides.

5. Serve immediately with tofu dipping sauce and a side of rice.

Tofu Dipping Sauce:

Ingredients:

4 T soy sauce	2 T white vinegar	2 cloves of garlic, crushed	1 tsp. sesame oil

Instructions: In a bowl, whisk all the ingredients together.

This creamy chicken soup is a favorite of one of my daughters.

Sopa: Mama's Chicken Noodle Soup
SERVES 4-6

Ingredients:

8-10 cups of your preferred broth (we usually make chicken broth)

1 onion, chopped

2 medium-sized carrots, julienne style

1 stick of celery, sliced thinly

1-2 cups of cabbage, sliced thinly

1-2 cups of cooked chicken, shredded (boil the chicken, let it cool and then shred with two forks or hands)

½ bag of elbow macaroni

Optional: ¼ cup of milk or cream

Instructions:

1. In a deep stock pan, heat 2-3 tablespoons of oil.

2. When ready, add the onion and cook until translucent.

3. Then add the stock.

4. Let the stock come to a boil and then add the chicken. Turn the heat down and continue to let it simmer.

5. In a separate frying pan, heat two tablespoons of oil.

6. When ready, add the carrots and celery. Stir fry until well cooked, but vegetables remain crisp.

7. Then add the cabbage and stir until cooked through. Season with salt and pepper.

8. When the vegetables are done, add them to the broth.

9. Then add the pasta and boil until it is cooked.

10. For a creamy soup, add the cream or milk at this point.

11. Season to taste.

The first time I asked my dad how to make munggo, he said "Just boil it all together." It didn't sound quite right, so I double checked with my mom and was glad I did.

Munggo (Mung Bean Stew)
SERVES 4-6

Ingredients:

1 cup green mung beans

5 cups water or your favorite stock (plus 2 more cups on reserve)

1 tablespoon vegetable oil

2 cloves garlic, minced

1 medium-sized onion, sliced

1 large tomato, diced

½ lb. shelled shrimps

1 cup of diced pork

1-2 tablespoons patis (fish sauce)

salt and pepper to taste

1 package of baby spinach

Instructions:

1. Rinse the beans and drain.

2. In a deep pot, combine the beans, water and season with some salt.

3. Let the water come to a boil and then reduce it to a simmer.

4. Allow the beans to cook for about an hour, or until soft or doubled in size.

5. In a large pan, sauté the garlic in oil, until golden.

6. Then add the onion.

7. When the onion has softened, add the tomato, pork and fish sauce or salt (if not using fish sauce) and pepper.

8. Cook completely through and then set aside.

9. When the beans are done, add the pork mixture to the pot.

10. If much of the liquid has absorbed, add another cup or two of water.

11. Cook for another 10-15 minutes.

12. Then add the shrimp and spinach. Boil for 2-3 more minutes.

13. Season to taste with salt, pepper or patis.

For a vegetarian option, omit the pork and shrimp and instead add some pan-fried tofu with the spinach. This can also be made with just pork or with only the addition of shrimp. It's entirely up to you!

Some refer to this dish as *Picadillo*, but in our home we always called it *Giniling*, which is a stew made with minced meat. Similar to *torta*, my family makes many different versions of *giniling*. Here is one of them...

Giniling
SERVES 4-6

Ingredients:

1- 1 ½ pounds of ground beef, pork or chicken

2 cloves garlic, minced

1-2 tablespoon(s) oil

1 bay leaf

1 medium onion, chopped

1 medium tomato, chopped

2 large potatoes, cubed

2 tablespoons soy sauce

½-1 cup water or enough to cover the meat

½ red pepper, diced

salt and pepper to taste

Optional: If you would like to try other vegetable options, you can also add ½ cup of green peas or ½ cup of diced carrots.

Instructions:

1. In a non-stick pan or skillet, cook the ground meat with a sprinkle or two of salt.

2. When the meat has cooked, drain and set aside.

3. In a medium pan, heat and when ready add oil.

4. Sauté garlic until golden.

5. Then add onion and stir quickly.

6. Then add the tomato and cook until both are soft.

7. Then add the meat, potatoes, bay leaf, soy sauce, water, salt and pepper. Cover and let it boil. (If using carrots, add them here.)

8. When it comes to a boil, bring it down to a simmer and cook for about 20-30 minutes, or until the potatoes are cooked.

9. When the dish is almost done, add the red pepper or peas. Cook for a few more minutes.

10. Season with salt and pepper to taste. Then serve immediately with jasmine rice.

This tangy soup filled with vegetables can be combined with meat or seafood, and is one of the dishes I often cook during the winter season. There are versions made with tamarind which provides that sour punch, but my family uses lemons instead to capture that flavor. *Sinigang* always reminds me of my grandma who regularly made it using shrimp. Although this recipe features salmon, it's almost just like Grandma's!

Sinigang na Isda
SERVES 4-6

Ingredients:

10 cups of water

2-3 cloves of garlic, minced

1 medium onion, chopped

1 medium tomato, chopped

Juice from 3 lemons or 1/2 cup of lemon juice

2-3 salmon fillets, chopped in half or any other type of fish you like

*1 bunch of radish, peeled if you like and chopped in half

1 cup trimmed green beans

1 eggplant, sliced in rounds

3-4 cups spinach

1-2 green hot peppers (optional, add for some spice)

*There are actually of variety of other vegetables that can be used in this dish. I grew up enjoying okra in my family's *Sinigang*. It's my favourite vegetable and I would ask my mom to always add extra. Long string beans called *sitaw* are the usual type of string bean used and *kangkong*, a green leafy vegetable common in the Philippines would be used instead of spinach. The vegetables used in this recipe are what I am able to find locally and work well as substitutes.

Instructions:

1. Heat a large stock pot and add a tablespoon of oil when ready.

2. Sauté the garlic, onions and tomatoes together.

3. When soft, add water and lemon. Let it to come to a boil.

4. When the water begins to bubble, bring it down to a simmer and add all the vegetables, except for the spinach. For a spicy soup, add green pepper here.

5. When the vegetables are tender, add the fish.

6. After the fish is cooked, add the spinach. Let it cook for another two minutes or until the spinach has wilted.

7. Adjust the seasonings: salt, pepper, *patis* or add more lemon juice if needed.

8. Serve immediately with jasmine rice and a small bowl of 1T *patis* and 1T lemon juice mixed together for more of a sour punch.

DID SOMEONE SAY PARTY?

The next few recipes are the ones I associate most with our family celebrations. These are just a small sample of what would appear on the table during birthdays, Christmas or other special occasions. For me, it is never a true party without any of these dishes!

Mama's Filipino Macaroni Chicken Salad
SERVES 6-8

Ingredients:

1 package of elbow macaroni

1-2 pieces of cooked and cooled chicken breast

2 carrots, peeled and diced

2 celery sticks, diced

4 tablespoons of sweet relish

1 can of pineapples, drained and chopped

1 scallion, minced

1½ cup to 2 cups of mayonnaise (depends on how creamy you would like the salad to be)

Salt and pepper to taste

Instructions:

1. Cook the macaroni according to the package in a pot of salted water. When done, drain and set aside.

2. Shred the chicken into thin pieces.

3. In a large bowl, combine the macaroni and chicken with the rest of the ingredients.

4. Mix well.

5. Add salt and pepper to taste.

6. Refrigerate at least 1 hour before serving.

> Note: This is a sweet macaroni salad and my mom usually adds a ½ cup of raisins in her version. As a kid, I would remove the raisins and now, as an adult I choose to exclude them. Feel free to use raisins or not.

Making *lumpia (eggrolls)* is a true labor of love. I remember our family working together in the kitchen, chopping vegetables and later rolling the *lumpias* up. We would make batches of *lumpia* and freeze them for later. When the *Lolos* (grandparents) visit, my children often look forward to making *lumpia* with them.

Lola's Vegetable and Tofu Lumpia
MAKES 36 LUMPIAS

Ingredients:

Lumpia Filling:

4 medium carrots, (about 2 cups) peeled and sliced julienned

8 to 10 ounces (about 2 cups) green beans, trimmed on the ends and thinly sliced on a diagonal

10 ribs of celery (about 2 cups), sliced thinly

1 medium onion,(about 1 cup) diced

1/2 large head green cabbage with outer leaves discarded, (about 6 cups) sliced thinly

2 large sweet potatoes, (about 5 ½ cups) peeled and julienned

5 large cloves garlic (about 2T) minced

4 blocks of tofu, drained and sliced into thin rectangles.

2 to 3 tablespoons soy sauce

1 teaspoon of freshly ground black pepper

*Alternatively, you could chop the vegetables using a food processor, but the cooking results could vary.

Lumpia Wrapper:

½ cup warm water

1 tablespoon flour or cornstarch

1 package of 36, 8-inch square and thin spring roll sheets (usually found in Asian grocery stores)

Dipping Sauce:

2 large cloves garlic, minced

¼ cup white vinegar

2 teaspoons soy sauce

Pinch sugar (optional)

Pinch of black pepper

For Frying:

2-3 cups of vegetable oil

Instructions:

For the filling-

1. When the vegetables are prepared, heat 3 tablespoons of oil in a non-stick frying pan.

2. When ready, fry some slices of tofu and cook until golden. Fry the rest of the slices in batches.

3. When cooked, stand the tofu upright in a colander lined with a paper towel, to release the excess oil and allow it to cool down.

4. While the tofu rests, heat a wok or shallow pan over medium-high heat. Add garlic and cook for 2 minutes, stirring, until the garlic is fragrant, but not burned.

5. Lower the heat, add onions and cook for 5 minutes, stirring until it has softened.

6. Then add the cabbage and celery, cook for 15 minutes more, continuing to stir the mixture.

7. Add the sweet potato and cook for 10 minutes or until softened, continue to stir the vegetables.

8. Afterwards, add the carrots and green beans and let the mixture cook for another 10-12 minutes.

9. While the last of the vegetables are cooking, chop the tofu into small cubes and then add it to the mixture.

10. Add the soy sauce and black pepper. Mix well and cook until all the vegetables are tender.

11. When done, season to taste and allow the filling to cool.

12. While the filling rests, make the paste and prepare the wrappers for the *lumpia*. Mix the warm water and flour/cornstarch together until you get a slightly thin pasty texture.

13. Open the package of wrappers and separate the wrappers, one by one. Carefully pull them apart and stack them, alternately as square and diamond shapes, on a plate. Cover with a clean, damp dish towel until ready to use. Prepping them this way will help speed up the rolling process.

Usually there are visual instructions on the back of every egg roll package that demonstrates how to roll *lumpia,* but just in case, here's how to assemble them:

14. Place 1 wrapper down on a plate. It should rest in a diamond shape with one corner pointing towards you. Place a tablespoon of the filling about 2 inches above the corner closest to you and with your hands, spread it out into a mini log. Lift the corner closest to you and fold it over the filling. Tuck it snugly against the vegetables and tofu, so the corner lays flat.

15. Roll the wrapper twice, then neatly fold in the left and right-hand sides of the wrapper. Roll once again from the bottom, then dip your fingers into the paste and use them to dampen the remaining edges of the wrapper. Roll the lumpia as tightly as possible, ending with the far corner of the wrapper. The *lumpia* should be about 4 inches long. Place the rolled *lumpia* in a single layer on a plate and cover with plastic wrap or wax paper. Repeat.

16. When you are ready to cook the *lumpia*, line a colander with several layers of paper towels. Heat the canola oil in a medium saucepan.

17. Fry a few *lumpia* at a time until crispy and golden brown. If the oil is heated properly, it should take about 2 1/2 minutes for the *lumpia* to brown on both sides. Transfer the *lumpia* to the lined colander when they are done. Repeat.

For the sauce: Whisk together the garlic, vinegar and soy sauce in a small bowl. Serve alongside the *lumpia*.

If you don't want to cook all the *lumpia* at once, feel free to freeze them. If there is a lot of the filling left over, you can also freeze it for next time!

Typical party foods that we enjoy on special occasions: Chicken Macaroni Salad and *Lumpia*

Almost Filipino

Pancit Canton with Tofu
Serves 6-8

Ingredients:

14-16 oz package of Pancit Canton noodles

2 cloves of garlic

1 onion, chopped

2 carrots, julienned

2 celery sticks, sliced thinly

½ head of napa cabbage, sliced thinly

1 block of tofu, diced

3 tablespoons of vegetable oil

2 cups of vegetable broth

2 tablespoons of light soy sauce, separated

1 tablespoon oyster sauce

salt and pepper for extra seasoning

sliced lemon wedges

Instructions:

1. Heat a large, deep non-stick pan and add two tablespoons of oil.

2. When ready, add the tofu.

3. Fry until crispy and pale yellow.

4. Scoop tofu out with a slotted spoon and set aside.

5. Add the remaining tablespoon of oil and garlic.

6. When garlic turns slightly golden, add onions.

7. When the onions are transparent, add the carrots and celery.

8. Cook for about 5 minutes before adding the cabbage.

9. Then add 1 tablespoon of soy sauce, 1 tablespoon of oyster sauce, salt and pepper and stir fry.

10. The vegetables should remain crisp, but tender. Cook for another 3-4 minutes.

11. When done, remove and set aside.

12. In the same pan, add the broth, remaining tablespoon of soy sauce and a little bit of salt.

13. When the liquid comes to a boil, gently add the noodles.

14. The noodles will absorb the liquid and soften.

15. When the noodles are done, add the vegetables and tofu to the pan.

16. Continue to carefully mix all the ingredients together. Add salt and pepper or adjust any other seasonings to your taste.

Serve warm with lemon wedges on the side.

There are many variations of this dish. Here are some other ways to enjoy pancit canton:

For pancit with chicken: boil ½lb chicken breast and shred into pieces. Add with the vegetables.

For pancit with pork: boil ½lb pork and cut into thin slices. Add with the vegetables.

For *pancit with shrimp*: peel ½lb shrimp and boil separately. Then add it to the vegetables.

Growing up, *pancit* was the ultimate birthday party food. As kids, we were told to search for the longest noodle to eat, so that we could live a long life!

Pancit with tofu, chicken and shrimp.

Pops' Hamon (usually prepared the night before serving)
SERVES 8-10

Ingredients:

1 large cured pork butt on the bone

1 bottle of beer

½ container of pineapple juice

1 liter bottle of 7/UP or Sprite

2 bay leaves

½-1 cup of brown sugar (depends on how large your ham is)

Sliced pineapple rings

Maraschino cherries

Parsley

Instructions:

1. In a large pot, place the ham and bay leaves with the rest of the liquid ingredients.

2. Let the marinade come to a boil and then turn the heat down.

3. Let the ham simmer for 30 minutes, rotating halfway.

4. Afterwards, cover the pot and let it sit overnight.

For the next day...

5. Preheat oven to 400°F.

6. Place ham in a large roasting pan.

7. Using a pastry brush, glaze the ham completely with the marinade.

Almost Filipino

8. Then rub the ham with brown sugar. Make sure it is evenly coated.

9. Bake for 30 minutes.

10. When cool, garnish with sliced pineapple rings, maraschino cherries and parsley.

SWEET CRAVINGS

These are three of my favorite Filipino sweet treats. They can be enjoyed after a meal or for *meryenda* (mid-afternoon snack).

Almost Filipino

My daughters love to make these sticky rice cake treats! By the time they reached elementary school, they could make them on their own!

Palitaw (Coconut Sesame Rice Cakes)
SERVES 6-8

Ingredients:

1 cup sweet rice flour

1/4-1/2 cup water

1 cup grated coconut

1 cup sugar

½ cup toasted sesame seeds

Instructions:

1. Heat oven to 350°F degrees and toast sesame seeds until golden. When cooked, set aside and allow it to cool.

2. In a large bowl, using a wooden spoon or rubber spatula, mix in the flour with the water. Bring together until it forms into a firm ball. You may have to add a little more water or flour to achieve the right texture.

3. Boil a quart of water in a deep pot, then bring it down to a simmer.

4. Take a spoonful of dough and place it in your hands. Roll the dough into a little ball and then flatten it down the middle. Make 3-5 of these rice patties at a time.

5. Drop the rice cakes in the water. Be sure to keep them from crowding. When they float to the top, they are ready. Remove them with a slotted spoon.
(This should take about 30-50 seconds)

6. Place on a wire rack and allow a few minutes to cool.

7. When the rice cakes are cool enough to handle, roll them in coconut.

8. Repeat with the rest of the batter.

9. In a small bowl, combine the sugar and sesame seeds together.

10. When ready to eat, sprinkle this combination on top of the *palitaw*.

Serve with the sugar/sesame topping on the side, for added sweetness!

Lola Precy's Leche Flan
(CAN BE MADE UP TO A DAY IN ADVANCE)
SERVES 6-8

Ingredients:

¼ to ½ cup of sugar

8 egg yolks

1¼ cups of condensed milk

1½ cups of evaporated milk

1 tsp vanilla extract

1 tsp grated lime zest (optional)

Instructions:

1. Preheat the oven to 325°F.

2. Pour sugar in a 6" round baking tin or aluminum foil dish. (Or *llanera,* the type of pan usually used in the Philippines to make *leche flan*)

3. Over a low flame, hold the pan over the heat and let the sugar caramelize. This can take a few minutes. *This is the trickiest part of the recipe.* As the sugar is melting, swirl the pan around, to evenly coat the bottom and the edges of the pan. When done, set aside to cool. (Alternatively, you can also melt the sugar in a pot over low heat, then pour it into the pan. Swirl the liquid around to cover the pan completely.)

4. In a bowl, combine the egg yolks, the condensed and evaporated milks, along with the grated lime zest and vanilla. Stir and combine the ingredients well.

5. Pour into the baking pan. Cover pan with foil.

6. Using a larger baking or roasting pan that can hold the flan, fill it halfway with water and place it on the middle rack of the oven.

7. Then lay the flan inside the steam bath.

8. Bake for 1 hour or until firm.

9. When done, let cool and refrigerate for at least 2 hours before serving.

10. When ready, slide a knife around the sides to loosen up the flan. Lay a serving platter on top of the flan. Then with one hand firmly holding the platter, carefully flip the *flan* over to display the beautiful caramelized top and let the syrup fall along the sides. Garnish with mint or berries.

Next to *Ube,* this was **the** favorite cake of my childhood that was often baked by one of my dad's four sisters. Don't let the long list of steps keep you from making this cake. It's super easy and deliciously worth baking!

Tita Babe's Mocha Roll
SERVES 6-8

Ingredients:

Cake:
1 tsp. instant coffee

1 tsp. hot water

6 egg whites

6 egg yolks

¾ cup sugar

¾ cup flour

½ tsp. vanilla

Mocha Buttercream:
½ cup butter, softened

½ cup confectioner's sugar

1 tsp. instant coffee

1-3 tablespoons of cream

Instructions:

Preheat oven to 350°F.

Cake:

1. Line a large jelly roll pan with parchment paper or grease it with butter and sprinkle with flour.

2. Dissolve coffee granules in a drop of hot water and set aside.

3. In a medium bowl, beat egg whites on high until they are stiff, about 2-3 minutes.

4. In another large bowl, combine egg yolks and sugar. Beat on high for 2 minutes. Set aside.

5. Then add the coffee and vanilla extract. Beat for another minute.

6. After the mixture appears creamy, sift the flour over it and stir until well combined.

7. Then fold in the egg whites and carefully blend all the ingredients.

8. Gently pour the batter into the pan and spread the mixture evenly with a spatula.

9. Place the pan in the center of the oven and bake for 15 minutes.

10. Meanwhile, have a clean tea towel ready.

11. When the cake is done, run a knife along the edges to loosen it up from the pan.

12. Lightly sprinkle the cake with some icing sugar and cover it with the tea towel.

13. Quickly invert the pan onto the counter.

14. Remove the pan and peel off the parchment paper.

15. Starting from the narrow end, begin to roll up the cake with the tea towel.

16. Let the cake sit in this position for at least 20 minutes or until the cake has cooled completely.

17. When the cake is ready, carefully unroll the cake.

18. Using a spatula, spread a thin layer of the cream all over the cake.

18. When the cake is evenly covered, roll it up again without the towel. Then with a serrated knife, trim the ends off.

19. With the seam of the cake facing downwards, lay the cake on a serving platter. Cover the rest of the cake with the leftover frosting and decorate.

Filling/Frosting:

1. Dissolve granules in a drop of hot water and then stir coffee into the cream. Set aside.

2. With an electric mixer, cream the butter well.

3. Then with the mixer on, slowly begin to add a spoonful of sugar at a time, combining well before adding the next spoonful.

4. After the sugar has been added, keep the mixer on and slowly add the coffee/cream mixture, tablespoon by tablespoon. To prevent curdling, allow the liquid to be well absorbed before adding the next spoonful.

Acknowledgements

I would like to thank my family-Ma, Pops, G.G., the Titas, Puba and Dee Dee- for all the love and support throughout the years and for all the beautiful meals that brought us together. May we continue to be blessed with many more moments around the table. For mi amor, Jesús, *graciés* for all your love, for always giving me the space to pursue my dreams and for being my number one taste tester. To Tala and Pau, my inspiration for the book, thank you for the gift of being your mama and for being the best helpers in the kitchen! *Mahal kita-mga anak ko*! To my dearest friends (Prague Fam) for letting me test out my dishes on you- thank you for your appetites! AB & NH-The Prague Basket, where all the writing started! HE, MH & MM-thanks for the extra set of eyes and advice. BB-This wouldn't have come alive if you hadn't set the path, TY. A special thanks to the Tiny Book Course for the guidance and encouragement to make this book happen.

About the Author

Liezel de La Isla is an educator and cooking enthusiast. Born in NYC to Filipino immigrants, she has lived in New York City, Washington D.C. and Milan, Italy. She currently resides in Prague, Czech Republic. Liezel enjoys reading cookbooks, spending time in grocery stores and making waffles for her kids on the weekends, but not necessarily in that exact order. She began her culinary journey in the kitchens of her family and recently completed the Leith's School of Food and Wine Essential Cooking Certificate. This is her first cookbook, though probably not the last. Find more of Liezel's recipes at: zelicious.club and @zel.i.cious on Instagram.

INDEX

Appetizers:
Lumpia, 29

Desserts:
Leche Flan, 41
Mocha Roll, 43
Palitaw, 39

Main Dishes:
Arroz Caldo, 16
Chicken Adobo, 11
Chicken Salad, 28
Giniling, 23
Hamon, 36
Munggo, 21
Pancit Canton, 33
Sinigang na Isda, 25
Sopa (Chicken Noodle Soup), 19
Tofu, 18
Torta (Omelette), 13
Torta Special, 14

Side Dishes:
Rice, 8
Sinangag (Garlic Fried Rice), 9

www.ingramcontent.com/pod-product-compliance
Lightning Source LLC
Chambersburg PA
CBHW082336300426
44109CB00046B/2507